Audit Report

Report Number: OIG-SBLF-12-002

SMALL BUSINESS LENDING FUND: Soundness of Investment Decisions Regarding Early-Entry Institutions into the SBLF Program

Report Date: February 17, 2012

Office of Inspector General

DEPARTMENT OF THE TREASURY

Contents

Audit Report 1

Results in Brief 2

Background 4

Treasury Approved Institutions that May Have Difficulty Meeting Repayment
and Dividend Obligations 6

Treasury Used a Flawed and Untested Credit Analysis Methodology to
Predict Applicant Repayment Ability 16

Recommendation 18

Management Comments and OIG Response.. 18

Appendices

Appendix 1:   Objectives, Scope, and Methodology 25
Appendix 2:   Management Comments.. 27
Appendix 3:   FDIC and FRB Comments 31
Appendix 4:   Major Contributors.. 36
Appendix 5:   Report Distribution 37

Abbreviations

FBA   Federal Banking Agency
FDIC   Federal Deposit Insurance Corporation
FRB   Federal Reserve Board of Governors
OIG   Office of Inspector General
SBLF   Small Business Lending Fund

OIG

The Department of the Treasury
Office of Inspector General

Audit Report

February 17, 2012

Don Graves, Jr.
Deputy Assistant Secretary for Small Business, Housing, and Community Development

This report presents the results of our audit of investment decisions involving banks admitted to the Small Business Lending Fund (SBLF). SBLF is a fund created to provide capital to community banks with assets of less than $10 billion with incentives to stimulate small business lending. Our audit objective was to determine whether the initial group of institutions approved for participation in the SBLF program was financially sound and able to meet SBLF repayment and dividend obligations. Our audit focused on 23 of the first 55 participants approved for funding and on Treasury's implementation of the investment decision process. To further evaluate the effectiveness of the decision process, we followed up on our previous report recommendation that Treasury obtain more robust information from the appropriate federal regulators on the financial health of institutions seeking funding.

To accomplish our objective, we reviewed documentation supporting Treasury's investment decisions and interviewed SBLF staff, officials from two of the federal banking agencies (FBAs)—the Federal Deposit Insurance Corporation (FDIC) and the Federal Reserve Board (FRB)—and Treasury's third-party financial analysts. We also compared FBA supervisory consultative memoranda to the most relevant bank examination reports from the FBAs to determine whether they provided Treasury with robust and complete information regarding the financial health of applicants. We did not obtain reports of examination from state regulators because state laws prohibit the sharing of reports of examination with non-regulatory entities.

We conducted our fieldwork from July 2011 through January 2012 in accordance with Government Auditing Standards. Those standards require that we plan and perform the audit to obtain sufficient, appropriate evidence to provide a reasonable basis for our findings and conclusions based on our audit objectives. We believe the evidence obtained provides a reasonable basis for our findings and conclusions based on our audit objectives. Appendix 1 contains a more detailed description of our audit objective, scope, and methodology.

Results in Brief

While Treasury intended to approve only those institutions that could meet SBLF program dividend and repayment obligations, our review of 23 approved institutions disclosed that 12, or 52 percent, had significant supervisory issues that could restrict their ability to meet their financial obligations to the SBLF program. Although the banks reviewed had CAMELS composite ratings of "2," Federal bank examiners and, in some cases, supervisory consultations noted multiple supervisory concerns about bank earnings, asset quality, and management. However, FBAs did not always report concerns identified in bank examinations, leaving Treasury without sufficiently robust information about the financial condition of institutions seeking funding. Although Treasury designed a program that targeted financially viable institutions, it did not specify the types of supervisory information requiring disclosure in FBA consultations as we had previously recommended. As a result, FBAs exercised significant discretion when disclosing supervisory concerns, and may have considered mitigating factors differently.

In other cases, where Treasury was informed of supervisory concerns prior to investment decisions, we found no evidence that Treasury considered such issues in its approval decisions. For example, Treasury's investment staff appropriately questioned whether 8 of the 12 institutions would be able to pay Treasury dividends on SBLF securities, and noted that 2 of the 8 may have to use SBLF funds and/or borrow money to finance SBLF dividends and/or bank operations. However, Treasury approved these institutions without a clear rationale, including three that had repayment probabilities below program thresholds and one that was under a dividend restriction by its regulator. Treasury's Investment Committee overrode the repayment analysis results because the initial probabilities were considered to be too conservative. This constituted a deviation from Treasury's credit analysis process, and in every case reviewed by the audit, appeared to be done to increase each bank's chances of approval. Finally, Treasury used a flawed and untested credit analysis methodology to predict applicant repayment ability.

The weaknesses identified raise questions about whether Treasury negotiated an effective supervisory consultative process, considered sufficient information, and consistently implemented its investment decision process. Also, without evidence of how supervisory concerns raised in the consultative process were addressed in Treasury's final decision, it is unclear whether some of the institutions approved in June 2011 have the fiscal ability to consistently meet their dividend obligations and repay principal as the Small Business Jobs Act intended. Because the investment period for the SBLF program has passed, we did not recommend improvements to the investment decision process. However, we are recommending that Treasury create an internal watch list and engage in enhanced monitoring of the 12 banks with supervisory issues identified by our audit.

Management Response

In a written response, Treasury provided comments on the report findings and identified planned corrective actions to implement the report recommendation. Management's response is summarized in the Recommendation section of the report, and the text of the response is included in Appendix 2.

Because our report refers to the FBAs' role in the investment decision process, we provided the FDIC and FRB with a draft of the report for comment. In written responses, the FDIC and FRB generally disagreed with the report's assertion that they did not fully disclose concerns reported in bank examinations. Both agencies downplayed the significance of the supervisory issues identified and stated that they believed the OIG did not give adequate deference to the composite CAMELS "2" ratings of the banks reviewed. Further, the FDIC commented that the report intimated it was obligated to report every supervisory finding, which Treasury had not directed it to do, and such findings were expected to be remediated in the normal course of business. The FDIC also contested any criticism of their supervisory consultation memorandum's lack of detail on commercial real estate concentrations. Finally, the FDIC disagreed with the report's suggestion that enforcement actions were lifted to qualify banks for the SBLF program, and FRB expressed concern with the amount of information disclosed from its confidential supervisory reports. The full text of FDIC's and FRB's responses is included in Appendix 3.

OIG Comment

OIG believes that Treasury's corrective actions are responsive to our recommendation. With respect to Management's comments, OIG maintains its concerns that Treasury made decisions without being able to fully document that it adequately considered all of the risks of investing in the applicants. In addition, we continue to believe that

Treasury gave too much authority over the information it would receive to the FBAs.

With respect to the disclosure of supervisory issues by the FBAs, the OIG provided FDIC and FRB with specific examples of supervisory issues that were not reported to Treasury, which the agencies acknowledged were not disclosed in their supervisory consultative memoranda. The report makes clear that the OIG believes Treasury had responsibility for specifying the information it needed, and does not state that the FBAs deliberately withheld information or had an obligation to report all supervisory findings. The report also notes that Treasury had access to CRE concentrations through other data sources. We disagree, however, that all of the undisclosed issues had either been resolved or were insignificant. For example, one of the "2" CAMELS-rated banks, for which deteriorating asset quality was a concern, continues to have deepening asset quality issues. As of September 30, 2011, the bank had nearly doubled its provisioning for loan and lease losses, while total non-current loans and leases had increased by almost 800 percent over the same period. The OIG also disagrees that the CAMELS ratings should have been sufficient for Treasury's review. CAMELS ratings are not only susceptible to becoming stale, but OIG and FDIC OIG reports have found that CAMELS ratings do not always reflect the full risks of an institution. Further, in the SBLF process the FBAs stated that their supervisory consultations did not provide any forward-looking validations of viability, and only reflected information as of the date of the assessment. These limitations on CAMELS ratings should have led Treasury to request additional information in order to make fully-informed investment decisions.

Where appropriate, we have revised the text of the report to address the FDIC's concerns about the termination of enforcement actions and to incorporate technical corrections suggested by both FDIC and FRB. The OIG has also carefully obscured specific identifying information about the approved banks while maintaining sufficient detail to maintain the integrity of the audit and compliance with Government Auditing Standards.

Background

On September 27, 2010, President Obama signed into law the Small Business Jobs Act of 2010, establishing the SBLF. SBLF is a fund created to provide capital to community banks with incentives to stimulate small business lending and, as a result, promote job creation and economic growth within communities. In addition to statutory eligibility requirements, participation in the SBLF program was restricted to financially viable institutions that were (1) adequately capitalized, (2) not expected to become undercapitalized, and (3) not expected to be placed into conservatorship or receivership.

Treasury launched the SBLF program in December 20, 2010, and by the June 22, 2011 application deadline, had received requests from 935 financial institutions for $11.8 billion of the $30 billion authorized for the program. By the program's September 27, 2011 funding deadline, Treasury had disbursed $4.03 billion to 332 institutions. Treasury made the first investment decisions in June 2011, approving 55 institutions. The remaining approvals occurred in the last quarter of the fiscal year, and Treasury disbursed the majority of the funds in the last month leading up to the September 2011 deadline.

In May 2011, we reported that Treasury established an 8-step investment decision process that examined applicant eligibility, financial viability, and ability to repay Treasury's SBLF investment.[1] Two key components of Treasury's decision process were FBA validation of each applicant's financial viability and a credit analysis performed by third-party financial agents to determine applicant ability to repay Treasury's investment and meet SBLF dividend obligations. However, at that time, Treasury was still developing the process for evaluating applicant repayment ability. Our report disclosed that Treasury had designed the program to target institutions with sufficient capital to repay the SBLF investment and to increase small business lending. While we reported that the process was consistent with legislative eligibility requirements, we also identified areas for improvement. Specifically, we reported that Treasury did not require thorough disclosure from the FBAs of supervisory issues influencing the health of the banks and had granted FBAs significant discretion over the types of information they could report to Treasury. Further, we reported that Treasury's process did not provide for checking back with FBAs prior to closing on its SBLF investments to ensure that the financial condition of institutions had not changed since approval.

We recommended, among other things, that Treasury: (1) specify the types of information that must be in the supervisory consultative narratives provided by the FBAs; and (2) confirm with FBAs that there were no changes in the institution's financial viability or supervisory information prior to disbursement of SBLF funds. Treasury personnel did

---

[1] OIG-SBLF-11-001, *Small Business Lending Fund: Investment Decision Process for the Small Business Lending Fund*, May 13, 2011.

not agree to specify the types of supervisory issues that FBAs should report, or to change procedures to confirm with FBAs whether changes in the financial condition of institutions had occurred, because doing so would have reopened what had already been lengthy negotiations with the regulators. However, Treasury told us that they ultimately confirmed that there were no changes in the financial viability of an institution before funding.

Treasury Approved Institutions that May Have Difficulty Meeting Repayment and Dividend Obligations

Our audit disclosed that 12, or 52 percent, of the 23 institutions reviewed have significant supervisory issues that could make them unable to fully meet their financial obligations to the SBLF program. Although we do not conclude that Treasury inappropriately approved these institutions for SBLF participation, records of Treasury's decisions do not clearly show how or if Treasury officials considered some of the risks of these investments. Federal bank examination reports, CAMELS[2] ratings, and/or supervisory consultative memoranda showed concerns about bank earnings, asset quality (such as commercial real estate exposure at 300 or more percent of total risk-based capital[3]), and inadequate bank management. Reports by FBAs and the Treasury Office of Inspector General (OIG) have shown that these characteristics can contribute substantially to the financial decline of banks. Even if these supervisory issues do not affect a bank's viability, they may impair a bank's ability to consistently pay dividends or repay Treasury's investment. For example, commercial real estate loans typically require 100 percent risk weighting, requiring a bank to retain more capital to meet regulatory capital requirements and reducing liquidity needed to meet an institution's financial obligations to Treasury.

---

[2] "CAMELS" refers to ratings of six essential components of an institution's financial condition and operations that FBAs assign to financial institutions. These component factors address: adequacy of capital; quality of assets; capability of management; quality and level of earnings; adequacy of liquidity; and sensitivity of the institution's earnings or capital to market risk. FBAs assign composite and component ratings of 1 to 5, with 1 indicating the strongest performance and least degree of supervisory concern; and a 5 indicating the weakest performance, and highest degree of supervisory concern.

[3] Regulatory guidance establishes that, among other measures, a bank has a commercial real estate concentration when total commercial real estate loans represent 300 percent or more of the institution's total risk-based capital (excluding loans on owner-occupied property). The outstanding balance of the institution's commercial real estate loan portfolio must also have increased by 50 percent or more during the prior 36 months.

In some cases, bank regulators did not fully disclose supervisory concerns relevant to Treasury's decision, and may have considered mitigating factors differently. This occurred because FBAs had significant discretion over the type of supervisory information to provide Treasury. When questioned about why all supervisory issues were not disclosed, FDIC stated that many of the supervisory issues were resolved by ensuing state examination reports, which it could not release to us as their disclosure is restricted by state law. Further, FDIC explained that the undisclosed issues, while important to bank management, had no impact on the viability of the institutions. FRB stated that the supervisory issues were already reflected in the CAMELS ratings provided to Treasury. We believe such issues were important because OIG and regulator reports have shown that some of this supervisory information can indicate risky lending practices or poor risk management. Further, the CAMELS ratings are static and the FBAs would not validate future predictability of future financial losses. For this reason, we previously recommended that Treasury request more robust information about supervisory issues, such as an institution's compliance history, enforcement actions taken against it, and matters requiring attention identified in bank examination reports. Treasury, however, declined to implement the recommendation because it believed that FBAs already understood the types of information they needed to report, and they did not want to reopen what had been an already lengthy negotiation process with the FBAs.

Treasury Did Not Obtain Sufficiently Robust Information from FBAs About the Condition of Financial Institutions Applying for Funding

FBA supervisory consultative memoranda used for SBLF investment decisions frequently did not fully disclose supervisory concerns noted in bank examination reports for 11 of the 12 institutions. The "supervisory validation of viability" section of the supervisory memorandum instructs FBAs to provide a narrative of material supervisory issues, including ongoing financial conditions and enforcement actions, if any. The instructions also required discussion of any CAMELS component ratings lower than "3," but did not specify that all supervisory issues should be disclosed. As described below, the examination reports contained a variety of supervisory issues that we believe might have been relevant to Treasury's investment decision, but were not reported by FBAs. Specifically, the memoranda omitted discussion of credit risk information for three banks and management problems for four banks. This occurred because Treasury did not provide FBAs guidance on the types of supervisory concerns to be addressed in the consultative memoranda as we previously recommended.

Treasury informed us that they were aware of the high commercial real estate concentrations based on information from other data sources, but with a few exceptions were not aware of the significant management issues flagged by the regulators in their bank examination reports. Treasury heavily relied on the CAMELS management component rating assigned by the FBAs when evaluating management's effectiveness. Almost all of the banks in our sample received "2" ratings in management. Some of these banks, however, had management issues flagged in bank reports of examination or reported in supervisory consultation memoranda that, while they might not have affected the CAMELS rating, should have been relevant to Treasury's decision.

Below are examples of institutions for which there were undisclosed or partially disclosed supervisory concerns about earnings performance, asset quality and management:

- The supervisory memorandum for one bank disclosed that it had a "2" rating in asset quality, but did not mention its commercial real estate concentrations or the increasing credit risk associated with its portfolio. According to the relevant examination report, the bank had a commercial real estate concentration of almost 450 percent of total risk-based capital. The bank also had negative retained earnings in one of the prior three examination periods.

    Additionally, the memorandum did not disclose multiple matters requiring board attention that examiners raised in the relevant examination. Each matter on its own was not significant; however when considered collectively, they indicated that bank executives were having difficulty managing the bank overall. Because Treasury was not aware of these issues, it relied on the "2" rating the bank received for management from its FBA and the supervisory memorandum reference that the applicant was a "well-managed bank."

- For a second bank, the FBA's memorandum omitted discussion of the bank's commercial real estate concentration. According to the relevant examination report, the bank's commercial real estate concentration to total capital ratio was nearly 500 percent, with non-owner-occupied commercial real estate at around 350 percent, representing high exposure to a risky sector.

    The bank also had multiple undisclosed matters requiring attention, calling into question management's ability to effectively manage daily operations of the bank. Key among these were inaccurate call reports and improper methodologies for calculating its allowance for loan and lease losses and managing liquidity effectively. Because the FBA did not disclose these concerns, Treasury relied on management's "2" rating assigned by the FBA and the state regulator's observation that the bank had no enforcement actions.

- An FBA reported that a third bank, a de novo,[4] had negative retained earnings, which could lead to the state supervisory agency restricting dividend payments. The FBA, however, did not disclose that the bank's commercial real estate exposure increased from 60 to almost 250 percent of Tier 1 capital since the last exam. Further, the FBA did not report that commercial real estate lending was the bank's primary strategy or that the loan policy approved for the bank allowed commercial real estate lending concentrations of up to 700 percent of total capital. Finally, the FBA did not disclose that the bank had three recent board resignations, and that in the most recent exam poor director attendance at board meetings constituted a matter requiring board attention. Treasury relied on the "2" rating the FBA had assigned to the bank's management.

Without access to the underlying supervisory information, Treasury relied on CAMELS ratings and other positive statements in the supervisory consultative memoranda to evaluate the effectiveness of bank management, and did not obtain further information from the FBAs.

In writing their consultations for Treasury, FDIC officials told us they often had access to updated state examination and supervisory information about SBLF applicants showing that the specific supervisory concerns had been satisfactorily resolved. FDIC officials said that other information, such as a de novo bank's rapid asset growth or poor earnings, was normal and did not need special mention. FDIC officials also stated that they used their supervisory judgment about whether to include the specific facts we identified, and there was no effort or intent to mislead Treasury as to the supervisory condition of any of the SBLF applicants they regulated. However, because state law precludes the sharing of state regulatory information, we could not verify whether supervisory concerns omitted from the consultative memorandum had been satisfactorily resolved. Finally, the FRB told us that because CAMELS ratings already reflected supervisory concerns involving the banks it regulates, additional discussion was unnecessary.

---

[4] A de novo bank is one that has been in operation for 7 years or less.

Supervisory Issues Noted Should Have Been Cause for Concern

Previous Treasury OIG and FBA reports have shown that poor asset quality, poor risk management, and passive bank boards of directors can contribute substantially to the decline of a bank. The Federal Reserve Bank of St. Louis has reported that deterioration in asset quality often first shows up in a bank's earnings as they begin to provision for potential loan losses, which occurs well in advance of other financial health indicators.[5] Bank management's risk tolerance is also critical. For example, Treasury OIG reported that La Jolla Bank management's pursuit of a high-risk lending strategy led the institution from average or above average CAMELS ratings to failure.[6] Similar management strategies of risky lending practices and poor risk management also contributed to Partners Bank's decline and ultimate failure.[7] In fact, FBAs regard bank management, which is the governance capability of an institution to identify, measure, monitor and control the risks of an institution's activities and to ensure safe, sound, and efficient operations, as the most important element for successful operation of a financial institution.

These types of bank weaknesses may not mark a bank as a problem bank, but they do raise concerns about whether institutions with these issues have the fiscal ability to carry on operations, pay SBLF dividends and repay SBLF principal as the Small Business Jobs Act intended.

FBAs Had Discretion over What Supervisory Issues to Report

In May 2011, we reported concerns that the supervisory memorandum used in the SBLF review process allowed the FBAs significant discretion on the type of information to provide Treasury. The memorandum allowed FBAs to provide discussion of material supervisory issues in the form of supporting comments in a narrative. We noted that while the information requested may have been sufficient under the process established for the Troubled Asset Relief Program because the FBAs were recommending institutions for funding, it was not sufficient for SBLF because Treasury was making the investment decisions. Therefore, we recommended that Treasury explicitly request more robust information to be reported in the FBA consultative memoranda.

---

[5] Federal Reserve Bank of St. Louis, *Earliest Indicator of Bank Failure Is Deterioration in Earnings*, Spring 2010.
[6] OIG-11-086, *Safety and Soundness: Material Loss Review of La Jolla Bank*, FSB, July 14, 2011.
[7] OIG-11-084, *Safety and Soundness: Material Loss Review of Partners Bank,* July 14, 2011.

Treasury Admitted Institutions Despite Supervisory Issues and Investment Staff Concerns about Applicant Repayment Ability

In many cases, Treasury had negative supervisory information prior to making investment decisions, and approved institutions without considering such information or clearly documenting the bases supporting its decisions. Even without the supervisory information, Treasury personnel questioned whether 8 of the 12 institutions would be able to pay Treasury dividends on SBLF securities, including one whose regulator had restricted it from paying dividends. Treasury also approved three institutions with repayment probabilities below program thresholds and two institutions that Treasury correctly noted would have to use SBLF funds and/or borrow money to pay SBLF dividends and/or finance bank operations. For example:

- One de novo bank had less-than-satisfactory earnings ratings in two of its last three exams. Although the capital levels for the bank appeared to be satisfactory, examiners had concerns with the high risk the bank carried. Commercial real estate exposure was almost 300 percent of total risk-based capital, excluding owner-occupied commercial real estate. Just over half of the bank's loan portfolio was concentrated in approximately 30 loans to very few borrowers in a volatile sector. As of September 30, 2011, the bank had reduced its commercial real estate from the prior year, but had nearly doubled its provisioning for loan and lease losses, while total non-current loans and leases had increased by almost 800 percent over the same period.

  Additionally, the FBA disclosed that past strategic planning had been inconsistent, and that not only were there no plans to raise capital, but the bank also planned to reduce capital. In addition, deteriorating asset quality might constrain the bank's ability to effectively engage in small business lending. The consultative memorandum further disclosed that problem loan identification was weak, and that in an effort to reduce overhead, the bank fired its chief credit officer and had no intention of filling the position. The memorandum also said that the absence of a chief credit officer contributed to the increase in adverse classifications and non-accrual loans. When it evaluated this bank, Treasury relied on the "2" rating the bank received for management from its FBA.

- Treasury approved a holding company that, according to its FBA, reported under $20,000 in cash as of December 31, 2010. As a result, the holding company will heavily rely on its subsidiary bank to service the SBLF dividend payments. The bank currently has positive retained earnings, although the most relevant exam reported that bank earnings are not sufficient to fully support operations, adequately fund the bank's allowance for loan and lease losses, and maintain required capital levels. The bank also had negative retained earnings for the last three bank examinations and a less-than-satisfactory earnings rating from its FBA in each of those exams. Additionally, the supervisory consultative memorandum indicated that capital levels at the bank are realizing declining trends that would worsen should asset quality continue to decline. The bank's loan portfolio is heavily concentrated in commercial real estate, which comprises almost 375 percent of its Tier 1 capital, in excess of regulatory guidelines. This leaves the bank disproportionately exposed to downturns in the commercial real estate market, which continues to experience poor values and recovery. Additionally, the bank's "other real estate holdings," representing loan foreclosures, grew from $0 in 2009 to almost $2 million as of December 31, 2010.

Treasury explained that although they were aware of the subsidiary bank's "3" CAMELS rating in earnings, it expected that, as a de novo bank, earnings would increase over time. The bank also had almost $5 million in securities available for sale and net income of nearly $200,000 per year. Further, Treasury officials told us they were not concerned about the bank's declining asset quality because its non-performing assets were within reasonable limits and the bank had received a "2" CAMELS rating in asset quality. However, the current level of non-performing assets would increase as asset quality continues to decline.

Treasury's disregard for the bank's "3" CAMELS rating for earnings and reliance on the bank's "2" CAMELS rating for asset quality put inconsistent emphasis on the two CAMELS ratings and discounted supervisory comments. We believe that Treasury should not have disregarded the earnings rating since future earnings are particularly uncertain for de novos. Additionally, Treasury should have been more skeptical of the high rating in asset quality, given that asset quality for de novo banks starts high until the portfolio matures and experiences more defaults.

- Treasury admitted a second holding company that had debt on trust-preferred earnings representing almost 50 percent of its capital, which a subsidiary bank completely serviced. In addition to servicing the trust-preferred dividends, the subsidiary bank was to be the primary source for payment of SBLF dividends as well as for a multi-million dollar note for an airplane the holding company purchased in 2010.

Although the bank's regulator reported the bank's capital as being satisfactory, it noted that the bank needed additional capital to meet growth targets. The bank received less-than-satisfactory ratings in earnings for the prior three examination periods. The most relevant exam noted that the bank continued to struggle with limited earnings mainly because of a declining net interest margin that required the bank to reduce interest rates on loans. The bank had also experienced a rise in problem assets, which significantly increased its loan loss reserves and the bank's overhead costs. According to Treasury's Investment Committee memorandum on the bank, past due loans deteriorated at the beginning of 2011, "hinting at additional asset quality issues still to come."

Instead of relying on the "3" CAMELS rating the subsidiary bank had received in earnings, Treasury stated that it believed the bank had a more than sufficient level of earnings. According to the FBA, earnings trends were improving, and would allow the bank to service its obligations, including SBLF securities. In addition, prior year bank earnings had exceeded holding company debt service obligations for SBLF funding at the highest dividend rate.

Treasury also noted that capital was "2"-rated and that the bank had raised additional capital subordinated to Treasury's funding. Treasury also observed that asset quality was "2"-rated, non-performing loans were below 3 percent of total loans, and non-performing assets were less than 2 percent of total assets. Therefore, Treasury viewed classified assets as manageable.

We believe that Treasury should not have discounted the bank's historical struggle with earnings performance by focusing on recent, short term improvements in earnings. Although the bank reported positive net operating income during the first part of 2011, as of September 30, 2011, it was again negative, declining by nearly 200 percent over the prior year. Additionally, the bank's rise in problem assets, coupled with its proposed reduction in interest rates on loans, were clear indicators that the bank's earnings might not be stable. In fact, by September 30, 2011, retained earnings had decreased over 600 percent from the prior year and were negative. Further, we believe that Treasury had indications that asset quality, although rated a "2," would decline in the future. Based on the Investment Committee memorandum, Treasury noted that recent improvements in the portfolio corresponded with significant net charge-offs and a simultaneous deterioration in loan loss reserves. Further, Treasury expected additional asset quality issues to develop. We note that as of September 30, 2011, non-current loans and leases had declined by nearly 50 percent, but provisioning for loan and lease losses had increased by nearly 400 percent. This would seem to indicate that the bank may be continuing to charge off its bad loans, while increasing its reserves for significant losses in the future.

- Treasury approved a third holding company even though its FBA had documented, in its supervisory memorandum, concerns about the company's asset quality, management, and ability to pay SBLF dividends. The holding company was heavily reliant on the dividends of its subsidiary bank for its cash flow, and therefore would have to rely on the bank's earnings or SBLF funds to meet its obligations under the SBLF program.

In September 2010, the state banking regulator rated the bank less than satisfactory in asset quality and management. It also noted that the volume of classified assets and past due loans had increased significantly. Bank management also needed to strengthen its credit risk practices and fund the allowance for loan and lease loss appropriately, resulting in a recommendation for a downgrade for the management rating. The bank's commercial real estate concentrations were high, at around 700 percent of total risk-based capital.

Treasury noted that while asset quality was a concern for the bank, the deterioration in assets resulted, in part, from the bank's acquisition of a failed bank with an FDIC loss-sharing agreement and from the economic downturn's impact on its commercial real estate portfolio. Further, although elevated, Treasury believed that classified assets were at manageable levels. They also observed that a portion of the bank's loan portfolio was government-guaranteed.

Treasury officials told us that they were not overly concerned about the management issues because they believed FDIC's willingness to let the institution acquire a failed bank is often an indicator that an institution is in good standing. Further, the bank's earnings, which are an indicator of management competency, were rated a "2" and were above average peer group earnings. Purchase of a failed bank, however, requires significant management efforts to integrate the acquired assets. According to the FDIC, many smaller institutions lack experience in working out problem credits and may not manage them effectively. Treasury, therefore, should have been more concerned about management capability and the CAMELS ratings downgrade in management.

As shown in Table 1 below, Treasury's investment staff correctly questioned whether 8, or 67 percent, of the 12 institutions with significant supervisory issues would be able to pay dividends on the SBLF securities. Treasury's financial analysts questioned the capacity of seven institutions to pay dividends and its investment analyst raised concerns about three. Additionally, Federal and state regulators raised concerns about three of the eight institutions whose repayment ability was questioned by Treasury staff.

Table 1: Reviewing Bodies that Questioned a Institution's Ability to Pay Dividends

Reviewing Body	Bank: 1	2	3	4	5	6	7	8	9	10	11	12
Federal Regulator			X		X	X						X
State Regulator												X
Financial Analyst	X		X			X	X		X	X		X
Investment Analyst			X					X				X
Investment Committee												

Sources: Institution Investment Committee Folios and the SBLF Investment Committee Minutes.

For example, the Investment Committee, which makes the funding recommendation:

- endorsed one institution that was under a dividend restriction imposed by its state regulator at the time of application to the program. Although its earnings were satisfactory for the examination report relevant to SBLF, the institution had negative retained earnings for 1 year prior to getting into the program, which was the basis for the restriction. Subsequent to approval, the restriction was lifted. According to information provided by the state regulator on February 23, 2011, the bank was currently unable to pay dividends because of negative retained earnings and could require both regulatory and shareholder approval before being allowed to make SBLF dividend payments.

- recommended a second institution based on it using SBLF funds to make the dividend payments. This applicant's primary bank was under an informal enforcement action and was restricted from passing on dividends to the applicant without prior approval from its federal regulator. Because the applicant had no operating income, it was dependent on the bank's dividends to pay its operating expenses, including SBLF dividends. As a result, the Investment Committee noted that the applicant could pay its SBLF dividends with part of its SBLF proceeds.

Treasury Approved Institutions with Low Repayment Probabilities

Treasury conducted a repayment probability analysis to evaluate the likelihood of applicants not repaying Treasury and established a probability of repayment of 80 percent as a requirement for program participation. However, it approved three institutions with repayment probabilities of less than 80 percent. The repayment probabilities for these institutions were 63 percent, 70 percent, and 76 percent. Two of the three institutions also required matching capital for investment approval.

Although Treasury analysts generally discussed whether institutions would be able to pay dividends on SBLF securities, the Investment Committee minutes and program documentation did not disclose why the committee recommended institutions for funding that were potentially unable to meet their SBLF obligations. Treasury informed us that the credit analysts often assumed a high level of charge-offs for classified assets, reflecting the analysts' lack of access to supervisory information. In its review, therefore, Treasury would often lower the projected level of charge-offs. For some institutions, Investment Committee meeting minutes seemed to indicate that committee endorsement was based on either raising an institution's qualitative scores or lowering projected charge-offs to bring each institution's repayment probability to the threshold for acceptance. For example, the committee noted that once the "qualitative factors are normalized" the score for one institution would increase to approximately 80 percent. For another, the minutes noted that the probability of repayment would be 80 percent if the institution wrote off all of its classified assets. The minutes for the third institution noted that Treasury increased the institution's repayment probability over what the analysts predicted by decreasing loan charge-offs. Consequently, Treasury did not review all the institutions in a consistent manner, since it waived the repayment threshold minimum for the three institutions. This gave the appearance that repayment probabilities were changed solely to increase each of these bank's chances for approval.

Treasury Used a Flawed and Untested Credit Analysis Methodology to Predict Applicant Repayment Ability

Treasury engaged two asset management firms to design a comparative repayment probability model to determine each applicant's likelihood of repayment relative to that of other community banks. This model provided Treasury with a forward-looking assessment of the applicants that were most and least likely to repay Treasury's investment out of all of the applicants. Yet, Treasury treated the results of the model as absolute probabilities and established a threshold of 80 percent for participation. Thus, an applicant assigned an 80 percent chance of repayment relative to other applicants could have an actual repayment probability that was much lower. Although the repayment probability was not the single determinant of whether Treasury approved an institution, it was a major factor in Treasury's investment decision.

Further, the repayment analysis required the analysts to rate applicants on 10 qualitative factors based on publicly-available information. The qualitative factors included commercial real estate concentration, reliance on deposit fees/debt interchange, interest rate risk profile, regulatory relations/business model considerations, structural funding profile, parent company liquidity, management strength, access to capital markets, financial strength, and cushion on traditional capital ratios. However, two of the factors were available only to the FBAs, and not to the analysts that were determining applicant repayment ability. For example, the analysts were required to rate the stability of each institution's management team and consider enforcement actions and similar regulatory concerns, but none of these items were publicly available. Additionally, because only 2 of the 23 institutions were registered with and reporting to the Securities and Exchange Commission, information was limited for the majority of the institutions, further making comparisons among the institutions difficult. Despite the lack of supervisory or public information, analysts told us they assigned scores to each factor to calculate each institution's probability of repayment. As a result, analyst judgment was responsible for a large part of the calculation.

The repayment methodology was also a formulaic, "one-size-fits-all analysis" that treated all applicants the same regardless of their size, age, and geographic location. For instance, the model assigned scores to applicants on quantitative and qualitative factors and weighted them for small de novo banks the same way as it scored them for large established regional community banks. However, de novo banks generally require stronger management in the early years for success, and therefore, management strength should carry considerably more weight in the analysis than was assigned. According to one regulator interviewed, the management strength factor should be weighted 50 to 70 percent of a de novo bank's score versus the 5 percent weight that was assigned. The financial analysts chose the weight assignments for each of the qualitative factors.

Further, Treasury's approach limited the factors considered, which did not allow adjustments to be made to reflect the nuances of different circumstances at different institutions. According to regulators, there is a multitude of factors that should be considered, including the supervisory history of the bank. However, a formulaic approach, where every factor is the same for each bank, does not allow the flexibility needed to interject judgment or consider additional information.

Whether Treasury's one-size-fits all repayment analysis methodology works for all banks is questionable because Treasury did not validate the predictability of the model before implementing it. According to the analysts, they often used this type of model in other applications, but they had never used it for determining the repayment probability of an investment. Because the model was new and had never been proven as predictive in other venues, placing heavy reliance on the model in the credit analysis of banks does not appear to be prudent.

Treasury officials explained that the Department tried to get the FBAs to perform the repayment analysis, but according to Treasury, the FBAs stated that they were not well-suited to that task, and Treasury was only able to get limited supervisory input with respect to the financial performance and management of an institution. The FBAs agreed to provide a viability assessment, but did not agree to predict the probability of loss of the SBLF investment or to validate the future viability of applicants, even though they had access to all supervisory information about the applicants.

Recommendation

Because the period of investment for the SBLF program has passed, we have not made recommendations for improving the investment decision process. However, we recommend that Treasury create an internal watch list and engage in enhanced monitoring of the 12 banks with significant supervisory issues. This will ensure that Treasury has an opportunity to make recommendations to the banks' management for improving their financial condition if it appears necessary.

Management Comments and OIG Response

On January 6, 2012, we provided Treasury with a draft of the report for comment. On February 6, 2012, Treasury submitted a formal response, which is contained in its entirety in Appendix 2 to this report. Management agreed to take the recommended action as part of its broader asset management process, and the OIG considers Management's proposed action to be responsive to the recommendation.

However, Management generally disagreed that it approved too many applicants and made decisions that were inconsistent and inadequately documented. Management also faulted the report for failing to acknowledge the satisfactory CAMELS ratings of the banks the OIG questioned, and for mischaracterizing Treasury's repayment analysis approach and treatment of supervisory issues. Finally, Treasury disagreed that FBAs may not have fully disclosed all significant supervisory issues to Treasury. Specific management comments on the report findings and our evaluation of them are summarized below.

Management Comment 1

Management asserted the report implies that Treasury should have been more conservative in reviewing and approving applicants, and that the program should have been cut in half. Management also disagreed with the report's conclusion that Treasury's process was inconsistent and not documented adequately, citing GAO's favorable description of its evaluation process.

OIG Response

The OIG disagrees with the inferences Management has drawn from the report. The report does say that Treasury made poorly-documented decisions that were based, in many cases, on incomplete information or inconsistent analysis. Also, in our view, Treasury's actions in some cases could be viewed as imprudent because it did not require sufficient information or address some of the investment risks. However, the report does not say or imply that Treasury should have cut the program in half. As Management admits, the report takes no position on whether Treasury appropriately admitted institutions to the program. Instead, the report finds that Treasury did not show or document that it was aware of or considered the full risks of its investments. In addition, the report addresses only half of the early-entry approved applicants, and the OIG findings apply only to the sample surveyed.[8]

In contesting the report's findings, Management also stated that members of Congress have suggested that Treasury's admission standards were too strict and that a larger pool of applicants should have

---

[8] Eliminating these 12 applicants from the 332 approved applicants would result in a reduction of only 3.6 percent.

been approved. However, we believe that outside pressure to admit or deny applicants is not a proper means for making good investment decisions. Further, we believe the small number of approved applicants instead likely reflects the unpopularity of the program. Of the 6,732 banks eligible for the program, a mere 935 applied. Based on data provided by Treasury, 307 withdrew voluntarily and 262 were statutorily ineligible or ineligible based on program standards. Of the eligible applicants that did not withdraw, Treasury approved 83 percent, suggesting that for eligible institutions, Treasury took a generous, not a conservative, approach.

We also believe that Management misinterpreted GAO's audit of its evaluation process and that its reliance on GAO's findings is misplaced. The GAO reported that Treasury established procedures to help ensure that applicants were evaluated consistently and were likely to repay funds.[9] In fact, an earlier report from our office came to a similar conclusion.[10] However, both of those audits focused on the design of Treasury's process. In comparison, this report examined the implementation of Treasury's process, and we found deviations from the process, vague documentation of decisions, inconsistent analysis, and incomplete information about applicants.

Management Comment 2

Management expressed concern that the report does not consider or acknowledge Treasury's Office of Financial Management's (OFM) forecast that the program will earn a profit for taxpayers and have smaller losses on individual investments.

OIG Response

OIG disagrees that it has not given consideration to OFM's forecast, because it addressed these projections in a prior report,[11] and concluded that Treasury's cost projection was overly optimistic. That report expressed concern that Treasury did not consider either historical retained earnings as an indicator of earnings performance or supervisory

---

[9] GAO-12-183, *Additional Actions Needed to Improve Transparency and Accountability*, December 2011.
[10] OIG-SBLF-11-001, *Small Business Lending Fund: Investment Decision Process for the Small Business Lending Fund*, May 13, 2011.
[11] OIG-SBLF-11-003, SMALL BUSINESS LENDING FUND: *Treasury Should Consider Supervisory Concerns Regarding Participant Management and Historical Retained Earnings When Estimating the Cost of the SBLF Program*, December 22, 2011.

concerns regarding participant management. Both factors could lead to a higher-than-expected default rate among participant banks, which could result in Treasury receiving less income than expected over the life of the program, thereby increasing program costs.

Management Comment 3

Management expressed concern that the report does not acknowledge that all 12 institutions received a composite "2" CAMELS rating from their FBAs, indicating they were fundamentally sound. Also, Management questioned why the OIG believed the 12 institutions had significant supervisory issues when their FBAs, who have a wealth of supervisory experience, gave them satisfactory CAMELS ratings.

OIG Response

The OIG agrees that the institutions in question were each assigned a composite "2" rating by their FBAs, which is mentioned in the text of the report. The report does not question the CAMELS ratings themselves, but suggests that the CAMELS ratings alone do not provide sufficient basis for making investment decisions. First, CAMELS ratings are static. They reflect the bank's information as of the quarter prior to the start of the examination. Some banks are examined as infrequently as every 18 months. Therefore, the CAMELS ratings can easily become stale. Treasury recognized this in its Capital Purchase Program (CPP) application process under the Troubled Asset Relief Program and assigned a presumptively higher level of scrutiny to banks with CAMELS ratings that were over 6 months old. Additionally, the FDIC has stated that "between examinations a bank's financial condition may change so that the CAMELS rating is no longer accurate." Secondly, and more importantly, the FDIC OIG has found that state and federal regulators do not always adequately assess risk in assigning CAMELS ratings. The CAMELS ratings represent the examiners' subjective assessments of the bank's condition. Finally, the FBAs were clear in their agreement with Treasury that their validation assessment would not predict future losses. As OIG and FBA reports have previously shown, supervisory concerns noted in bank examinations relative to asset quality, risk management, and the strength of a bank's board can contribute substantially to the decline of a bank.

Therefore, knowing that the CAMELS ratings were static and insufficient for predicting future losses, Treasury, as the investor, should have collected the additional information needed to determine whether the banks could repay its investment. Instead, by declining to require specific information from the FBAs and depending heavily on the CAMELS ratings, Treasury essentially left the fundamental decision to the FBAs.

Finally, we disagree with Management's inference that the OIG lacks supervisory expertise. The OIG has significant experience with evaluating the condition of individual financial institutions. The OIG is responsible for conducting material loss reviews that determine why individual banks fail. This has given the OIG substantial expertise on banking supervisory issues, particularly those that can materially impact the health of a bank.

Management Comment 4

Management states that the report's description of SBLF staff overriding the repayment analysis results and deviating from Treasury's credit analysis process is incorrect. Management also contests the report's observation that the purpose of the re-evaluation appeared to be to increase each bank's chances of approval, stating that the purpose was instead to give full and fair consideration to all applicants.

OIG Response

OIG disagrees with Management's characterization of the rationale for increasing the repayment probabilities because it is unable to substantiate Management's assertion. In the sample reviewed, Treasury established a participation threshold of an 80 percent repayment probability, and increased the repayment probability percentage for three institutions. The purpose may have been to give full and fair consideration to each applicant, as Treasury states, but the documents we reviewed did not support that. Instead, Treasury explained it made upward adjustments to normalize qualitative factors, or adjust assumptions about loan charge-offs. Further, the repayment probability appeared to be subject to prudential adjustments in only one direction: up, not down, and therefore gave the appearance that they were performed to aid the institutions.

Management Comment 5

Management stated that it was never Treasury's objective to approve only institutions with no supervisory issues. Further, in support of the program and Treasury's process, Management stated that all 332 institutions participating in SBLF—including the 8 institutions for which Treasury staff questioned the ability to pay dividends—have made the first dividend payments due under the program.

OIG Response

The OIG agrees with Management's description of the program, and congratulates Management on receiving the initial dividend payments. However, we do not believe that the payment of the first of 18 quarterly dividends over a 4½-year period is particularly predictive. As of February 15, 2009, only 8 out of the then 532 CPP participants had failed to declare a dividend payment to Treasury. By September 30, 2009, the number of CPP participants that had failed to declare a dividend had jumped to 38. Starting on December 31, 2009, the number of institutions missing dividend payments increased quarterly to 43, 67, 109, 137, and 155 before tapering off. By now, nearly 4 years into the program, 197 of the remaining 371 CPP participants have missed dividend payments. Therefore, in a similar program, institutions made early payments and then began to struggle to meet remaining obligations.

As stated in the report, OIG does not question Treasury's ultimate investment decisions. As Management notes, among the risks that Treasury discussed was the chance that some of the institutions admitted might struggle to pay dividends. Given the multi-year nature of the investment, Management's reliance on the payment of the first dividends does not address the report's concern that Management did not adequately consider long-term risks.

Management Comment 6

Management also disagrees with the OIG's contention that the FBAs may not have fully disclosed supervisory issues to Treasury.

OIG Response

OIG disagrees with Management's assertion, and is uncertain as to the basis for Management's statement. Management did not require specific supervisory information or ask for reports of examination that would inform it as to whether all supervisory issues were disclosed. However, the OIG compared the reports of examination to the supervisory consultative memoranda and identified multiple issues that the FBAs did not report to Treasury. The OIG then discussed these omissions with Management, which acknowledged that it was unaware of some of the information in those reports. Management may not agree that the information described was significant, but they did not receive it.

* * * * * *

We appreciate the courtesies and cooperation provided to our staff during the audit. If you wish to discuss the report, you may contact me at (202) 622-1090.

/s/

Debra Ritt
Special Deputy Inspector General for
Office of Small Business Lending Fund Program Oversight

Appendix 1
Objectives, Scope, and Methodology

We conducted the audit of the initial investment decisions for the Small Business Lending Fund (SBLF) in response to our mandate under section 4107 of the Small Business Jobs Act of 2010.[12] This section provides that the Office of SBLF Program Oversight is responsible for audit and investigations related to the SBLF program and must report at least twice a year to the Secretary of the Treasury and Congress on the results of oversight activities, including recommended program improvements.

We initiated our audit of the initial investment decisions on May 25, 2011. Our objective was to determine whether the initial group of institutions approved for participation in the SBLF program was financially sound and able to meet SBLF repayment and dividend obligations. Our audit focused on 23 of the first 55 participants approved for funding and Treasury's implementation of the investment decision process. To further evaluate the effectiveness of the decision process, we followed up on our previous report recommendation that Treasury obtain more robust information from the appropriate federal regulators on the financial health of institutions seeking funding.

To address the audit objective, we reviewed SBLF memoranda, charters establishing the Application Review Committee and Investment Committee, and memoranda of understanding between Treasury and federal banking agencies (FBAs). We also reviewed the Investment Committee folios for the 23 institutions, including Investment Committee Memoranda; Supervisory Consultation Memoranda from the FBAs;[13] the institutions' applications; third-party credit analyses; and a dividend self-certifications provided by applicants. Additionally, we reviewed the relevant reports of examination from each institution's FBA, Call Reports; Uniform Bank Performance Reports for the institutions; and Investment Committee and Application Review Committee minutes. We did not obtain reports of examination from state regulators because state laws prohibit the sharing of reports of examination with non-regulatory entities.

We interviewed SBLF program staff to gain an understanding of the application review process and Treasury's third-party financial analysts to obtain further clarification on the repayment probability calculation and credit analysis. We met with two FBAs—the Federal Deposit Insurance

---

[12] The Small Business Jobs Act of 2010, Public Law 111-240, was signed into law on September 27, 2010.
[13] FBAs for the 23 institutions were either the Federal Deposit Insurance Corporation or the Federal Reserve Board.

Appendix 1
Objectives, Scope, and Methodology

Corporation and the Federal Reserve Board—that reviewed the banks selected for our audit. We also interviewed another federal regulator to obtain its perspective on Treasury's SBLF application review process, including the repayment probability calculation and supervisory consultation request.

We conducted our fieldwork from July 2011 to January 2012 in accordance with Government Auditing Standards. Those standards require that we plan and perform the audit to obtain sufficient, appropriate evidence to provide a reasonable basis for our findings and conclusions based on our audit objectives. We believe that the evidence obtained provides a reasonable basis for our findings and conclusions based on our audit objectives.

Appendix 2
Management Comments

DEPARTMENT OF THE TREASURY
WASHINGTON, D.C. 20220

February 6, 2012

Debra Ritt
Special Deputy Inspector General for
Office of Small Business Lending Fund Program Oversight
U.S. Department of the Treasury
1500 Pennsylvania Avenue, NW
Washington, DC 20220

Dear Ms. Ritt:

Thank you for the opportunity to review the draft report by the Office of Inspector General (OIG) entitled *Review of Soundness of Investment Decisions Regarding Early-Entry Institutions into the SBLF Program* (the Report). This letter provides our official comment.

The Department of the Treasury (Treasury) appreciates the role of strong oversight of the Small Business Lending Fund (SBLF). Much of the feedback your office has offered over the past year has contributed to the design and implementation of the program, which has been a success. SBLF institutions already have made important progress toward achieving the goal of increasing small business lending. As of the third quarter of 2011, SBLF participants have increased their small business lending by $3.5 billion, or by 9.8 percent over baseline levels. These increases are widespread. Over 78 percent of all participants have increased their small business lending. Further, a substantial majority of participants—more than 60 percent—have increased their small business lending by 10 percent or more. And lending through the program has been widely distributed across the country. Banks and community development loan funds in 43 states and the District of Columbia have reported increased lending.[1]

In regard to the Report, however, we have numerous concerns. As an initial matter, the overall tenor implies that Treasury should have been more conservative in reviewing and approving applicants. For example, the Report concludes that over half of the first approved institutions that OIG reviewed had "significant supervisory issues."[2] The Report also claims that Treasury was unaware of issues that "should have been cause for concern," and it dedicates several pages to describing negative factors that Treasury should have considered more carefully.

We disagree with any suggestion that Treasury approved too many applicants. Cutting the program in half—as the report seems to propose—would have reduced the impact of the program

---

[1] *SBLF Fourth Quarter 2011 Use of Funds Report: Report Submitted pursuant to Section 4106(3) of the Small Business Jobs Act of 2010*, submitted to Congress on January 9, 2012.
[2] OIG reviewed 23 of the first approved institutions and concluded that 12 had "significant supervisory issues."

1

Appendix 2
Management Comments

dramatically. If anything, various Members of Congress have suggested that Treasury's process was too *strict*. They have argued that Treasury should have approved a larger, not smaller, pool of applicants. For example, Senator Jerry Moran recently noted that participation rates were lower than expected, suggesting that this may have been because "additional scrutiny, well beyond that contemplated by Congress, was employed in the [consideration] process."[3] Senator Carl Levin similarly stated that the main complaint he received was that Treasury implemented the SBLF program in "a very conservative way" to protect taxpayers—a way that made the program "less available to more banks."[4] The Report states that OIG does "not conclude that Treasury inappropriately approved these institutions for SBLF participation . . . ." In other words, OIG is not criticizing Treasury's ultimate investment decisions. Nonetheless, we believe the Report could mislead readers by suggesting that Treasury approved too many applicants.

The Report otherwise focuses on Treasury's process—rather than its investment decisions—and concludes that the process was inconsistent and not documented adequately. Again, we disagree. Treasury worked closely with the federal banking regulators to develop a review process that was robust in both design and implementation. Treasury confirmed each applicant's eligibility for the program, consulted with the relevant state and federal banking regulators, and performed a detailed financial assessment of each applicant. The assessments included, among other things, an evaluation of the institution's likelihood of repayment, a review of its small business lending plan, and an examination of sector analyses or current industry trend reports. Treasury also considered all supervisory consultation memos from an applicant's regulator, which described the institution's financial condition and performance. Ultimately, Treasury weighed these relevant factors and made considered judgments about each applicant.

There is strong evidence that Treasury's evaluation process was thorough and consistent. The Government Accountability Office conducted an in-depth review of the SBLF program and concluded that "Treasury adopted procedures to help ensure that applicants were evaluated consistently and were likely to repay funds . . . ."[5] In addition, Treasury's Office of Financial Management recently forecasted that the program as a whole will earn a profit for taxpayers and that losses on individual investments will be well below initial projections because Treasury approved institutions that were far stronger than originally anticipated. We do not believe that the Report adequately considers or acknowledges this information.

In addition, the Report contains a number of inaccuracies and omissions. We have listed below several examples that we raised in meetings with your team regarding its analysis of 12 approved SBLF institutions:

---

[3] U.S. Senate Committee on Banking, Housing, and Urban Affairs, Questions for the Record from hearing entitled *Financial Stability Oversight Council's Annual Report to Congress* (Oct. 6, 2011)

[4] U.S. Senate Small Business and Entrepreneurship Committee, hearing entitled *Review of the Small Business Jobs Act* (Oct. 18, 2011)

[5] GAO, *Small Business Lending Fund: Additional Actions Needed to Improve Transparency and Accountability*, GAO-12-183 (Dec 14, 2011)

Appendix 2
Management Comments

- The Report concludes that these SBLF institutions had "significant supervisory issues" that could hinder them from repaying Treasury. The Report fails to acknowledge that all 12 institutions were assigned a composite "2" rating by their federal banking regulators under the Uniform Financial Institutions Rating System. The definition of this rating states that "financial institutions in this group are fundamentally sound . . . [t]here are no material supervisory concerns."[6] Banking regulators have a wealth of experience evaluating the condition of individual financial institutions. It is unclear why OIG believes that these institutions had significant supervisory issues despite their satisfactory ratings from banking regulators.

- The Report states that SBLF staff "overrode" repayment analysis results and "deviat[ed] from Treasury's credit analysis process." This is not true. SBLF's documented policy was to make independent determinations for institutions that received differing assessments from third-party credit analysts and from banking regulators. Third-party analysts did not have access to confidential supervisory information. Accordingly, SBLF staff considered all available information in such cases and made independent decisions. The purpose of the policy was to give full and fair consideration to each applicant, not "to increase each bank's chances of approval," as the Report states.

- The Report concludes that Treasury "admitted institutions despite supervisory issues and investment staff concerns about applicant repayment ability." It was never Treasury's objective to approve only institutions with no supervisory issues. Instead, Treasury sought to construct a portfolio that reflected an overall risk level and program cost and that would achieve the dual objectives of increasing small business lending while also protecting the taxpayer's investment. In particular, the Report cites eight of the institutions and notes that staff questioned their ability to pay dividends. It is entirely appropriate in a robust investment process to discuss risk factors associated with potential investments. Ultimately, SBLF staff considered the investment risks cited in the Report along with other mitigating factors and recommended approval of each of the eight institutions. And to date, all 332 institutions participating in SBLF – including those eight – have made all dividend payments due under the program.

Finally, we disagree with your contention that the federal banking regulators may not have fully disclosed all significant supervisory issues to Treasury.

Despite our concerns, Treasury does not object to the Report's sole recommendation that Treasury "create an internal watch list and engage in enhanced monitoring" of the 12 banks included in OIG's analysis. While we disagree that these banks had "significant supervisory issues," Treasury agrees to take the recommended steps as part of its broader asset management process.

Thank you again for the opportunity to comment on the Report. We look forward to continuing our work together in the future.

---

[6] Federal Deposit Insurance Corporation, *Composite Ratings Definition List*, p. 6 (available at http://www.fdic.gov/regulations/examinations/ratings/FDIC_Composite_Ratings_Definition_List.pdf)

3

Appendix 2
Management Comments

Sincerely,

Don Graves Jr.
Deputy Assistant Secretary

Appendix 3
FDIC and FRB Management Comments

Federal Deposit Insurance Corporation
550 17th Street NW, Washington, D.C. 20429-9990

Division of Risk Management Supervision

February 7, 2012

Mr. Eric Thorson
Inspector General
Department of the Treasury
Office of the Inspector General
1500 Pennsylvania Avenue, NW
Washington, D.C. 20220

Re: OIG Draft Report captioned "Review of Soundness of Investment Decisions Regarding Early-Entry Institutions into the SBLF program."

Dear Mr. Thorson:

The FDIC appreciates the opportunity to comment on your draft audit report concerning the Small Business Lending Fund (SBLF) Program.

After reviewing the document in depth, the FDIC does not agree with some of the underlying premises and the general tenor of the draft audit report.

The role of the federal banking agencies, including the FDIC, in the SBLF process was to provide information to Treasury that Treasury could use in making its investment decisions. The FDIC did not make recommendations regarding whether Treasury should invest in any institution. The FDIC provided consultation memoranda with the most recent, relevant supervisory information available to us.

The draft audit report includes criticisms involving seven satisfactorily performing FDIC-supervised institutions that are rated '2' in the CAMELS rating system. The report suggests that the FDIC somehow misled Treasury into approving SBLF applicants that were, in the view of the Inspector General, unqualified for program funds. To the contrary, the FDIC followed the requirements of the law to consult with Treasury regarding its supervised institutions and carefully followed Treasury's consultation document instructions for the federal banking agencies. In no way did this agency misrepresent the facts to benefit participation by SBLF applicants.

Our overall impression from reading the draft report is that a reader would reach incorrect conclusions about the SBLF program and information supplied by the FDIC. Consequently, we do not believe that limited edits can address the fundamental concerns we have with the report. We have provided the attached redline which attempts to correct specific factual errors, and what we view as certain unfounded allegations with the hope that in addition to highlighting these specific concerns, your review of the entire document will help you better understand our overall concerns about the draft report.

We would like to highlight a passage from the report that illustrates our overall concerns. The draft audit report states:

Appendix 3
FDIC and FRB Management Comments

"While Treasury intended to approve only those institutions that could meet SBLF program dividend and repayment obligations, our review of 23 approved institutions disclosed that 12, or 52 percent, had significant supervisory issues that could restrict their ability to meet their financial obligations to the SBLF program...In some cases, however, Treasury did not have sufficiently robust information from the FBAs about the financial condition of institutions seeking funding or the FBAs did not fully disclose concerns reported in bank examinations...In some instances, regulators lifted enforcement actions prior to Treasury's investment decision, giving the appearance that the actions occurred to allow institutions to meet program eligibility requirements."

As noted above, the draft audit report refers to 12 institutions as having "significant supervisory issues." Seven of those institutions were state nonmember institutions supervised by the FDIC and state banking regulators with assigned CAMELS '2' ratings.

We disagree with the audit report's premise that comments contained in the exam report show that there were known, significant supervisory issues in these 2-rated institutions at the time the consultation memoranda were submitted. We also disagree with the implicit second-guessing of assigned regulatory ratings. Most obviously, a CAMELS '2' rating is indicative of a satisfactorily performing institution and such institutions are unlikely to have serious supervisory issues. Examination findings and recommendations at such institutions are generally expected to be remediated in the normal course of business. That was the case with the seven institutions cited. We also have significant concerns that the draft audit report takes comments in FDIC report of examination out of context, and does not consider the findings of state banking authority examinations that were completed between the time of the FDIC examination and the completion of SBLF consultation documents.

The audit report also criticizes our consultation memorandums' lack of detail on commercial real estate (CRE) concentrations. Importantly, information on CRE concentrations was readily available to Treasury through public data sources familiar to the SBLF program staff such as Call Reports, Uniform Bank Performance Reports, and public filings. Moreover, Treasury did not request the agencies to provide these data elements in consultations. In a number of the consultations which the FDIC provided throughout the process, CRE concentrations were discussed in detail where appropriate. There was no attempt by the FDIC to ignore or conceal CRE concentration information. Further, when Treasury had concerns about concentrations or other issues, they contacted us for more robust information which was provided.

We also have concerns with the audit report's findings relative to the termination of two enforcement actions at the time of institutions' SBLF application. As background, the FDIC initiates, modifies, and terminates a large number of enforcement actions each year, usually after the conclusion of an on-site examination. In the two cases of terminated actions that are cited in the audit report, both terminations followed recent examinations that reflected improvements at the subject institution. Further, one of the referenced actions was actually terminated by the state banking department, not the

Appendix 3
FDIC and FRB Management Comments

FDIC. The audit's suggestion that FDIC somehow acted to remove these enforcement actions to help applicants obtain SBLF funding is not warranted or factually justified.

For all FDIC-supervised SBLF program applicants, we provided Treasury's SBLF program office the most recently available *relevant* supervisory information regarding program applicants in consultation memoranda, including information from state examinations. The draft audit intimates that the FDIC was obligated to report every individual supervisory finding from previous examination reports (which we would consider outdated in many instances). Conversely, Treasury directed the federal banking regulators to concisely summarize the most current relevant supervisory information on applicant institutions in consultation narratives. The FDIC followed Treasury's instructions. Accordingly, outdated or less relevant supervisory information that may have been discussed in prior examination reports (as described in the audit) was not catalogued in the consultation memoranda.

The suggestion in the draft audit report that the existence (or lack thereof) of supervisory concerns could not be verified by the Office of the Inspector General because the FDIC did not provide state bank examination reports is misleading. The FDIC does not have the authority to disclose state bank regulators' examinations as those materials are the property of the appropriate state agencies. Any requests for such reports should have been made directly to the state banking agencies.

In view of these concerns that reach to the premise and tenor of the draft audit report, we believe that substantive narrative changes are needed beyond the comments we are providing in the redline edits. FDIC staff would be happy to discuss these issues in further detail at a convenient time.

Sincerely,

Sandra L. Thompson
Director

cc: Debra Ritt
Special Deputy Inspector General for SBLF Oversight

Enclosure

Appendix 3
FDIC and FRB Management Comments

BOARD OF GOVERNORS
OF THE
FEDERAL RESERVE SYSTEM
WASHINGTON, D.C. 20551

DIVISION OF BANKING
SUPERVISION AND REGULATION

February 9, 2012

Mr. Eric Thorson
Inspector General
Department of the Treasury
Office of the Inspector General
1500 Pennsylvania Avenue, NW
Washington, D.C. 20220

Dear Mr. Thorson:

Thank you for the opportunity to comment on your draft report titled "Review of Soundness of Investment Decisions Regarding Early-Entry Institutions into the SBLF Program" (hereafter referred to as "the IG report"). As Federal Reserve staff discussed in a call with IG staff several days ago, the Federal Reserve has a number of concerns with the tone and substance of the IG report.

First, the IG report states repeatedly that federal banking agencies (FBAs) did not fully disclose concerns reported in bank examinations. As discussed with IG staff, the Federal Reserve provided Treasury with the information it requested and that would be relevant to the evaluation of the condition and prospects of SBLF applicants. On the call, IG staff acknowledged that the Federal Reserve provided all requested information, and we believe that point should be clearly stated in the IG report. IG staff also suggested on the call that other information from supervisory reviews was not always included, and that point is made in the report. Moreover, the IG report goes further and implies that the FBAs deliberately withheld information from Treasury out of a desire to assist troubled banks. Certainly, insofar as the Federal Reserve is concerned, this suggestion is completely without foundation. The Federal Reserve was fully forthcoming with information to the Treasury staff running the SBLF program and provided all information requested by SBLF program staff.

Second, the IG report appears to wrongly place more importance on the descriptive observations contained in examination reports than on the overall ratings that those reports assigned. As a result, the IG report seems to fault Treasury staff for approving SBLF investments while overlooking what the IG report considers to be warning signs of serious financial or other difficulties contained in examination reports. We disagree both with the importance placed by the IG report on these examination observations, and on the conclusions drawn from them. The rating a bank receives on a CAMELS component takes into account the

Page 1 of 2

Appendix 3
FDIC and FRB Management Comments

various descriptive observations that underlie the rating on that component, and it is the rating itself that summarizes overall supervisory judgments regarding that factor. Thus, in our view, the Treasury SBLF staff's reliance on the rating and the information provided in the supervisory consultation memorandums was appropriate. The descriptive information contained in examination reports (such as the existence of matters requiring attention related to bank administration for a bank with a "Management" component rating of 2) should not be used to undermine the overall supervisory judgment of the bank's management in assessing the strength of the organization. Because the IG's conclusions appear to be based, at least in part, on a misreading of the findings in examination reports, the conclusions the IG draws from those reports should be revisited.

Finally, the Federal Reserve continues to believe that the IG report reveals too much information derived from confidential supervisory reports. Given that certain institutions are discussed in the report in considerable detail, readers may have — or believe they have -- enough information to identify these institutions, particularly since the IG report identifies the sample as 23 of the first 55 institutions approved under the SBLF program. Since the information provided in the IG report is drawn from examination reports and is generally negative toward the institution, speculation about which institution is being discussed can be very damaging, particularly without the benefit of seeing the broader context in the entire examination report. This kind of examination-related information is highly confidential, which is why we provided examination materials to the IG subject to confidentiality provisions. We do not believe that inclusion of this detailed and sensitive information is necessary to make the points the report addresses, and ask you to consider removing more of this highly sensitive material from your report.

The Federal Reserve is providing specific edits designed to address some of these concerns, but to fully address them we believe more thorough revisions may necessary. We appreciate the opportunity to comment on the draft report and would welcome the opportunity to meet with you and your staff to discuss our comments in greater detail.

Sincerely,

Maryann Hunter
Deputy Director

Appendix 4
Major Contributors

Debra Ritt, Special Deputy Inspector General
Lisa DeAngelis, Audit Director
Audrey Delaney, Audit Manager
Elizabeth MacDonald, Attorney
Bobbi A. Paulson, Referencer

Appendix 5
Report Distribution

Department of the Treasury
Deputy Secretary
Office of Strategic Planning and Performance Management
Office of Financial Management
Office of Accounting and Internal Control

Office of Management and Budget
OIG Budget Examiner

United States Senate
Chairman and Ranking Member
Committee on Small Business and Entrepreneurship

Chairman and Ranking Member
Committee on Finance

Chairman and Ranking Member
Committee on Banking, Housing and Urban Affairs

United States House of Representatives
Chairman and Ranking Member
Committee on Small Business

Chairman and Ranking Member
Committee on Financial Services

Government Accountability Office
Comptroller General of the United States

www.ingramcontent.com/pod-product-compliance
Lightning Source LLC
Chambersburg PA
CBHW081804170526
45167CB00008B/3314